POETRY FROM THE HEART OF GOD

"A TRUE WORSHIPER"

MARIE E. WILLIAMSON

Order this book online at www.trafford.com
or email orders@trafford.com

Most Trafford titles are also available at major online book retailers.

 www.trafford.com

North America & international
toll-free: 844 688 6899 (USA & Canada)
fax: 812 355 4082

Our mission is to efficiently provide the world's finest, most comprehensive book publishing service, enabling every author to experience success. To find out how to publish your book, your way, and have it available worldwide, visit us online at www.trafford.com

ISBN: 978-1-6987-0900-0 (sc)
978-1-6987-0899-7 (e)

Print information available on the last page.

Trafford rev. 11/22/2022

POETRY FROM THE HEART OF GOD
"A TRUE WORSHIPER"

SHINE ON ME LORD FOR YOUR GLORY!
I LOVE YOU!

LIVE IN ME LORD

YOU ARE MY JOY

v

TABLE OF CONTENTS

Dedication

This book of poetry and its artistic influences is truly an inspiration from the Holy Ghost. I never know what was hidden inside of me until I had trials, tests, struggles, sickness, and loss of friends, and then God began to speak to me through poetry. Thank you, Lord Jesus, for loving me and for revealing your hidden treasures through me what a joy getting to know you on such a special and intimate level.

Jesus Is My Father!

One may ask the question why is Jesus your Father?

And I may answer because He created me.

One may ask me, why He loves me so, and I may say, because
He send His son Jesus Christ to die for my sins.

One may ask the question why did Jesus die for my sins?

And I may say, because He loves me so, and desire to give me eternal life.

That's why Jesus is my Father.

6/11/18
11:18 P.M.

What Would life Be Like
If God Did Not Create Men?

For one thing, there would be no wives! Certainly, one cannot have a wife without a husband. So, God knew what He was doing when He created men.

Second, there would be no offspring. Women cannot have children unless there is a man. So, God knew what He was doing when He created men.

Third, we would not know what the moon would look like if we did not have men, because Neil Armstrong, Edwin Buzz Aldrin, and Michael Collins were the first men to walk on the moon. So, God knew what He was doing when He created men.

Fourthly, we would not have Dr. Martin Luther King Jr. a father of 4 children and a social activist who led Civil Rights movements in the United States from the mid-1950s until his death by assassination in 1968. So, God knew what He was doing when He created men.

Men are incredibly significant because God created them to fill a gap in life that is just for them. Without men, there would be no families. So, God knew what He was doing when He created men.

Men keep families stable, united, encouraged, faithful, and loving. encouraged, faithful, trustworthy, and loving. Now you see why men are required in our society! Thank God for creating men like you.

Men of Strength and Courage

KING DAVID

1. **Who was King David?** A Biblical Israelite king and the first monarch of all the Israelite tribes. He was the father of Solomon, who built the first temple in Jerusalem. David was an important figure in Judaism, 'Christianity, and Islam.

2. **How did he display strength and courage during his time?** According to Samuel 17, Saul and the Israelites are facing the Philistines in the valley of Elah. David brings food for his elder brothers, hears that Goliath has defied the army of God and of the reward from Saul to the one that defeats him, and accepts the challenge.

3. **What is strength?** (advantages) The quality or state of being strong.

4. **What is courage?** (boldness, bravery) The ability to do something that frightens one.

IN LOVING MEMORY OF MY BELOVED
AUNT LINDA MCBEAN

MY BELOVED MOM AND AUNTY YOU ARE GREATLY MISSED BY ALL THOSE YOU LEFT BEHIND. THANKS FOR ALL THE LOVE, GRACE, AND COMPASSION YOU SHARED WITH US WHILE WE HAD YOU. YOUR SMILE ALWAYS BRIGHTENS OUR LIVES AND GIVES US HOPE AND STRENGTH. WE MISS THE ENCOURAGEMENT YOU OFTEN GAVE US TO MOVE FORWARD IN LIFE. WE LOVE AND MISS YOU SO MUCH, BUT YOU ARE WITH GOD, AND THAT'S WHERE YOU BELONG. YOU SERVE YOUR TIME WELL.

xviii

"OCEAN CITY"

If you are very HUNGRY for CRABS, try Ocean City N.J.

xx

SPECIAL THANKS

To EVANGELIST BEVERLY SMITH, a kind and nurturing mother in the gospel, one who exemplifies the true love of Jesus Christ. As an angel sent from God to encourage, influence, and reveal several of my God-given gifts to me. Evangelist Smith, I love you so much and thank God for you being such a SPECIAL GIFT TO THE BODY OF CHRIST ESPECIALLY TO ME IN MY TIME OF NEED.

AUNTY DELLY

I thank God for you AUNTY DELLY. You rescued me from the hands of my enemies when I was sick and being treated like a nobody at St Michael's Hospital in Newark, New Jersey. But God heard my prayer in the bathroom on the floor and delivered me with a SURPRISE, you. Although we spoke on the phone, we had not yet met in person. God used His dream that he gave me one night to bring us together with the Williamson family on the phone. However, you and Anna- Kay were the first ones I encounter, sent on a mission by God to deliver me, because my time was not yet. How can I ever thank you for the love and dedication, faithfulness, sincerity, compassion you showed to me upon our first meeting in the hospital, but in writing publicly? Thank you for the chicken soup you brought, and all that love I needed. That is why I am so blessed and still alive today. I love you.

MARGARET GORDEN

Thank you for encouraging and praying with me in my time of need. Margaret, you always call just when I need help. When I pray and, God says help is on the way, you were His help for me. You are just like an angel in your conduct. Thanks for your kindness and sincere prayers always for me and my family especially during my aunt Linda's passing 4/18/21. You made me laugh during my time of mourning and despair. I am grateful for your spirit of gratitude toward God and me, especially when you had a stroke and God used me to heal you. You called me years later, during the pandemic with such gladness and thankfulness. Just in time to bless my life when I was struggling with some issues, after which the Lord thrust me into a greater anointing because of your sincere prayers for me. The Lord answers all your prayers for me just like that. Thank you, Margaret for being wrapped up and tighten -up with Jesus just to bless me.

Nancy Krimm

I thank God for the day he allowed us to meet. You have been a mother, friend, and an angel to me. Nancy, you have been such a help in my life. Thanks for dropping off groceries on my pouch and driving me to school, interviews, the doctor, the bank, and Philadelphia without complaining. That is why when you told me you have COVID VIRUS. I went to the Lord and cried unto Him and remind Him of your KINDNESS towards me. I asked the Lord to bring you back home from the hospital for my birthday and He did. What I love most about you, Miss.

Nancy is that you always believed in my prayers and never doubted them. You always said, I know God heard your prayers, Marie. It always marvels me. You believed in the prayers I prayed to God without me even having to blink. I believe God sees your FAITH AND THAT'S WHY HE ALWAYS ANSWERED THE PRAYERS. When 7 of your family members tested POSITIVE for COVID-VIRUS, and I prayed and told you God said it was well "They were all coming home." You believed that's why God always blesses you, because you never doubt the prayers. I am so thankful to my LORD for blessing me with a SPECIAL FRIEND LIKE YOU. ALWAYS GIVING TO ME. "GOD SAID YOU ARE A GIFT TO ME."

PASTOR BEVERLY WILLIAMS

Thanks for my first opportunity to preach on your ZOOM platform on May 28, 2020. Thanks for your love and support with my first book to encourage me to talk about during one of your services. Although I did not speak on it, you spoke for me and promoted the book. Thanks for your motherly love when I was being opposed in ministry, you simply hugged me and said, "YOU ARE SO FULL OF THE HOLY GHOST". So those who were teasing me when I worshiped God did not matter to me because God sent His angel to comfort me. Thanks for all your prayers when I moved. You were such a tower of strength and a force to reckon with. You fought for me in the spirit in prayer and called my name out to God. You were even willing to come and get me two hours away when I needed a ride. With such love and compassion I am profoundly grateful for you in my life. Who knows what our mighty God is up to? We just have to trust Him and do as he says, and he will do the rest. And "Yes" be kind to each other.

BISHOP GALE LEE

Thanks to Bishop Lee, who is so GRACIOUS and SINCERE. Thanks for confirming that the Lord had given me a WRITING MINISTRY. When I was sick, God used you to minister to me about His call to ministry years ago. You could tell me that God has called me to a "Writing and Publishing Ministry" Amazingly before I could tell you that the Lord had blessed me to write two more books. What a special gift God has given you. Truly, God is mighty and using you.

PSALM 90: 1

Lord, thou hast been our dwelling place in all generations. Before the mountains were brought forth, or ever thou has formed the earth and the world. Even from everlasting to everlasting, thou art God.

PROVERBS 22: 22

Rob not the poor, because he is poor: neither oppress the afflicted in the gate, for the Lord will plead their cause, and spoil those that spoiled them.

WORDS TO MOTIVATE ONE INTO THEIR DESTINY

INGENUITY- is the ability to think creatively about a situation or to solve a problem cleverly. For example, if you want to build a boat out of toothpicks and win, you'll need a lot of ingenuity. (intellect is the Latin word for it) fast thinking, like athletes who find exciting ways to outwit their opponents to achieve victory.

CONFIDENCE - full trust; belief in the powers, trustworthiness, or reliability of a person or thing: We have every confidence in their ability to succeed.
Belief in oneself and one's powers or abilities; self-confidence; self-reliance; assurance: His lack of confidence defeated him.

Inspiration - an inspiring or animating action or influence:
1. One cannot write poetry without inspiration.
2. Something inspired, as an idea.
3. A result of inspired activity.
4. A thing or person who inspires.

MOTIVATION - the state or condition of being motivated or having a strong reason to act or accomplish something:
We know that these students have strong motivation to learn.

ORGANIZATION - the act or process of organizing or of being organized.

CREATIVITY - the state or quality of being creative.
The ability to transcend traditional ideas, rules, patterns, relationships, or the like, and to create meaningful new ideas, forms, methods, interpretations, etc., originality, progressiveness, or imagination:
the need for creativity in modern industry; creativity in the performing arts.

Detail- extended treatment of or attention to particular items.

Captivating – appealing, pleasing.

Prolific- plant, animal, or person producing much fruit or foliage or many offspring. Means a person is highly fruitful and productive.

Catapulting- To suddenly experience a particular state, such as being famous. The award for best actress means that almost overnight she was catapulted into the limelight.

Favorite Quotes from Some of the Most Influential People Who Ever Lived

Martin Luther King

Our lives begin to end the day we
become silent about things that matter.
Faith is taking the first step even
when you don't see the whole staircase.

Mother Teresa

"If you judge people, you don't have no
timed to love them."
"if you can't feed a hundred people,
then feed just one."

Maya Angelou- "I've learned that people will forget what you said, people will forget what you did, but people will never forget how you make them feel." (source www.goodreads.com)

xxx

Benjamin Franklin

"Better slip with foot than tongue. He that lies down with Dogs, shall rise up with fleas."

John G. Lake- "The reason for the resurrection is that the Kingdom of Christ is not to be in heaven entirely. It is to be in the world. Ant the Lord and Savior Jesus is Christ is to rule in this world. Consequently, while we live in this world, we will need a body like our Lord's — capable of existence over there. (source www.goodreads.com)

Marie E. Williamson

Express love to each other while one is a live because we don't know what tomorrow may bring. Give to others when you have it don't wait until you died to leave if has an inheritance. You may just die before them.

From Rag To Riches

9/2022
7:00 A.M.

From rag to riches.
From rags to riches.
From rags to riches I will go.
From rags to riches.
From rag to riches.
From rags to riches I will go.
God told me so.
God told me so
God told me so.
If I only believe
If I only believe
If I only believe
God told me so
From rags to riches I will go.
From rags to riches I will go.

Why Am I Black

2017
6:00 P.M.

Why am I Black, Lord Jesus?

Why are my trials so many, Lord Jesus?

Why I can't seem to accomplish the things I desire to do. No matter how hard I try?

Is it my Blackness? That's blocking and hindering me, my Lord?

Why am I Black Lord Jesus?

What did I do?

That has caused such suffering for me and my people?

Or is it You? Who is living in me the devil doesn't like?

Why am I Black Lord Jesus? Is it for a greater purpose?

Why am I Black Lord Jesus?

What did I do?

That has caused such suffering for me.

Or is it You? Who is living in me the devil doesn't like?

Why am I, Black Lord Jesus? Is it for a great purpose?

One I cannot see, my Lord.

Show me, show me

What I cannot see, so my Blackness will not stop and hinder me.

Who me, the Christ in me?

Reveal yourself to me

So, I can attain my destiny.

READER'S NOTE

_____

_____

_____

_____

_____

_____

_____

_____

_____

_____

11/28/2014

The Needs Of Others

What a delight to help those in need.

It brings such joy and release to give to those in need.

Fulfilling the need of others blesses my soul when they are satisfied.

I cannot help but give to God's wonderful people when there is a cry for help.

How about you are you willing to HELP?

PUTTING THE NEEDS OF OTHER'S FIRST

The Faces Of The Needy

<u>2014 4:00 P.M.</u>

They are of all color, race, and creed.

The language spoken are many.

At times, it is difficult to tell what one is saying.

But with a little patience the accent, is understood.

They made up a special part of the public.

Although, they are partly ignored and forgotten about by society.

These are the faces of the poor and needy.

9

The Needy In My Community

2014 5:00PM

I wish I could do more for the needy in my community.

I believe it's everyone's moral responsibility to help his or her fellow man in need.

One never knows what may befall them in life.

Life is a struggle and has it's difficulties. Anyone can become homeless at any moment.

I often think it could have been me when I go to feed the needy.

It is only God's grace and mercies that kept me off the streets of America.

Although the Lord has blessed me to achieve two-college degree,

I was unable to find work while in school and after I graduated.

It was skills I had prior to and after college that helped me to attain a low-income job.

Jobs, of course, that I was not so delighted to go to at times.

What do I, do when there is a cry for help?

I must have compassion and do whatever it takes to ease the hunger of my fellow men.

Even if it means giving away my last bread or dime.

READER'S NOTES

Humankind

2014 2:00 P.M.

I notice today how the faces of the poor and needy are getting younger every day.

It's hard to say what the problem really is today.

Many young men and women of all nationalities are without shelter and food.

They don't have a clue how they get their last meal.

Their only hope is to be fed and kept through the night.

These are our lost generations without hope and love.

Living a life without knowing what's wrong.

Without them, what will this great nation do seeing the baby
boomers are getting older and will soon retire.

Who will fill in for the retirees if our youths are lost and without hope.

Colors And Shapes

11/ 21, 2008

5:00 P.M.

Children are cute children are sweet.

They are like the rainbow.

You can count them one, two, three, four, five, and six.

Their smiles are the shape of orange, cheery, apple, and watermelon.

Children are cute children.

They are like a bowl of Jell-O.

You can count them seven, eight, nine, and ten.

And start all over again.

Christmas Song

6/2/2008 5:00 P.M.

Deck the halls with rounds of hollies, A B C D E F G.

Now the hall with rounds of boilies fa-la- la- la- la- la- la.

One, two, three, buckle my fee.

Four, five, six, pick up my sticks.

Deck the halls with love and hollies

Fa-la-la- la- la la.

Seven, eight, lay them straight.

Fa- la- la- la –la- la- la- la.

GOD IS MORE THAN ENOUGH

8/12/09 1:40 P.M.

GOD IS MORE THAN ENOUGH FOR ME.

GOD IS MORE THAN ENOGH FOR ME.

DURING LIFES STORMY SEA.

HOW MY GOD HAS DELIVERED ME.

GOD IS MORE THAN ENOUGH FOR ME.

WHEN OLD SATAN THROW HIS DARTS OF DESPAIR AT ME.

GOD IS MORE THAN ENOUGH FOR ME.

WHEN I AM LOST IN MY THOUGHTS,

GOD IS MORE THAN ENOUGH FOR ME.

DURING TRIAL, TRIBULATION, I MUST NOT COMPROMISE.

GOD IS MORE THAN ENOUGH FOR ME

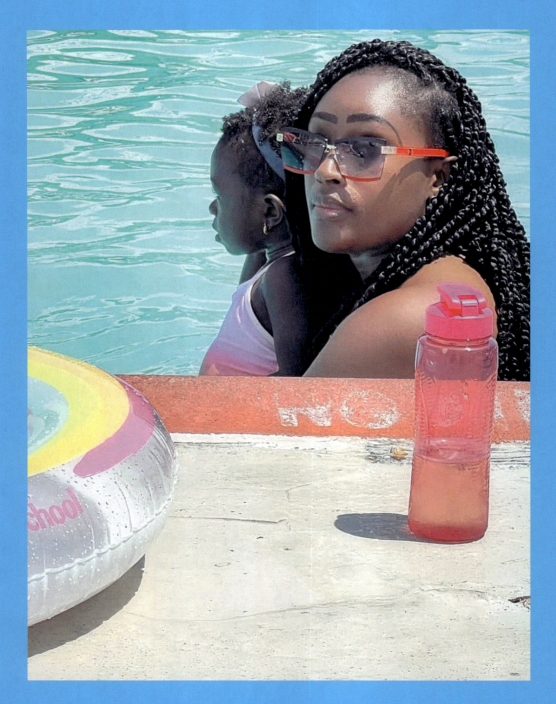

JESUS IS THE BISHOP OF MY SOUL

8/12/09

1:01 P.M.

JESUS IS THE BISHOP OF MY SOUL.

HE HAS WASHED AND CLEANSED AND MADE ME WHOLE.

JESUS IS THE BISHOP OF MY SOUL.

JESUS CARRIED ME WITH HIS HAND. AND FROM SINKING SAND HE HAS LIFTED ME UP TO STAND.

JESUS IS THE BISHOP OF MY SOUL.

JULY 8, 2008

"I LOVE YOU LORD"

I LOVE YOU LORD,
I LOVE YOU LORD,
I LOVE YOU LORD,
I LOVE YOU LORD
I LOVE YOU LORD.

ALWAYS AND FOREVER,

I NEED YOU LORD, I NEED YOU LORD, I NEED YOU LORD.

ALWAYS AND FOR EVER,

I PRAISE YOU LORD, I PRAISE YOU LORD, I PRAISE YOU LORD.

ALWAYS AND FOR EVER,

I ADORE YOU LORD, I ADORE YOU LORD, I ADORE YOU LORD.

ALWAYS AND FOR EVER,

GO BEFORE ME LORD.
GO BEFORE ME LORD.
GO BEFORE ME LORD.
GO BEFORE ME LORD.
GO BEFORE ME LORD.

ALWAYS AND FOR EVER,

GO BEFORE ME NOW, MY MASTER.
GO BEFORE ME NOW, MY SAVIOR.
GO BEFORE ME NOW, MY REDEEMER.

ALWAYS AND FOREVER.

I WILL MAGNIFIED THY NAME LORD,
LORD JESUS, BECAUSE I LOVE YOU.

ALWAYS AND FOREVER.
ALWAYS AND FOREVER.
ALWAYS AND FOREVER.

24

WRITTEN IN NEWARK, NEW JERSEY THE WINTER OF 2003 I NEED

DIRECTIONS AND ASKED THE LORD TO GO BEFORE ME. BECAUSE I SEEK
HIS GUIDANCE AND COUNSEL IN MY PATH TO DRIVE THE CAR. ALSO
PERTAINING TO ANYTHING I NEED TO DO. I ASKED GOD TO GO BEFORE ME

BECAUSE THEN HE PREPARES THE WAY FOR ME BEFORE I REACHED. YOU

SEE I ALWAYS NEED REASSURANCE AND CONFIRMATION, IN MY LIFE IN

ASKING THE LORD TO GO BEFORE ME, I WILL AND SHALL ALWAYS SEE HIS

DEVINE HAND WORKING IN MY LIFE.YES I ALWAYS DO BECAUSE HE

ALWAYS SHOWS ME HIS GLORY. JESUS SAYS TO ME "DO YOU SEE," I

SAID YES, LORD! AND LAUGH." "AND SAY THANK YOU JESUS." I LOVE YOU.

EVEN MORE, SO IN FLORIDA, YOU SEE DEAR READER THAT
WHERE I WAS HEADING. I LOVE YOU, MY BELOVED
LORD JESUS

"JE-SUS"

8/31/02

6:17 P.M.

JE-SUS, JE-SUS, JE-SUS, JE-SUS, JE-SUS, JE-SUS

YOU ARE THE ONE I ADORE.

JE-SUS, JE-SUS, JE-SUS,

YOU ARE THE ONE I ADMIRE.

JE-SUS, JE-SUS, JE-SUS, JE-SUS, JE-SUS,

I LOVE YOU JE-SUS,

JE-SUS, JE-SUS, JE-SUS,

I APPRECIATE YOU; I LOVE YOU.

JE-SUS, JE-SUS, JE-SUS.

JE-SUS, JE-SUS, JE-SUS.

THIS SONG WAS WRITTEN IN A HOSPITAL BATHROOM IN FLORIDA,
WHILE I WAS VISITING SISTER ARDRA, A MEMBER OF THE CHURCH I WAS
WORSHIPING AT. THAT'S WHEN JESUS REMINDS ME OF HOW MUCH I
LOVED HIM, AND HE GAVE ME THIS SONG TO WRITE.

ACTS

CHAPTER 18 VERSE 9 - 10
JESUS SAID TO ME BE NOT AFRAID, BUT SPEAK AND HOLD NOT THY
PEACE.
FOR I AM WITH THEE, AND NO MAN SHALL SET ON THEE TO HURT THEE:
FOR I HAVE MUCH PEOPLE IN THIS CITY.

2/17/08 7:50PM

"JE-SUS IS MY DELIGHT"

JESUS IS MY DELIGHT, IS MY DELIGHT.
JESUS, IS MY DELIGHT, IS MY DELIGHT.
JESUS, IS MY DELIGHT, IS MY DELIGHT.
IN THE MORNING, HE IS MY DELIGHT.
IN THE AFTERNOON, HE IS MY DELIGHT.
AT MIDNIGHT, HE IS MY DELIGHT.
HE IS MY DELIGHT, ALL THE TIME.
JESUS IS MY DELIGHT, IS MY DELIGHT.
JESUS IS MY DELIGHT, IS MY DELIGHT.

29

THIS SONG WAS INSPIRED AND WRITTEN ON JULY 31, 2003 BECAUSE JESUS
TOLD ME HE IS MY DELIGHT IN PSALM 16 VERSE 3.

"BUT TO THE SAINTS THAT ARE IN THE EARTH, AND THE EXCELLENT, IN WHOM IS ALL MY DELIGHT

A FAST, TUNE SONG AND CLAP."

2/21/08
7:00 A.M.

"OH YES, HE HEALED ME"

THIS MORNING WHEN I WOKE UP, I WAS SICK AND IN PAIN,

AND I CRIED OUT TO JESUS AND HE HEARD AND HEALED ME.

OH YES, HE HEALS ME!

JESUS HEALED MY BODY, MIND, AND SOUL.

OH YES, JESUS HEAL ME.

AND I THANK THE LORD FOR HEALING.

OH YES, JESUS HEAL ME.

OH YES, JESUS HEAL ME.

AND I THANK THE LORD, JESUS HEAL ME.

JESUS HEAL MY BODY, MIND, AND SOUL.

OH YES! JESUS HEAL ME.

OH YES, BY THE GRACE OF GOD JESUS HEAL ME.

OH, I THANK GOD JESUS HEAL ME.

OH YES, JESUS, HEAL ME.

OH YES, JESUS HEALED ME!

INSPIRED ON 8/15/08, BY MY LORD AND SAVIOR, JESUS IS THE GREAT PHYSICIAN.

HE DOES HEAL HIS CHILDREN, WHEN WE ARE SICK SPIRITUALLY OR PHYSICALLY. THE WORD OF GOD SAYS "HE WAS WOUNDED FOR MY TRANSGRESSION, HE WAS BRUISE, FOR MY INIQUITY THE CHASTISEMENT OF OUR PEACE WAS UPON HIM AND BY, HIS STRIPS WE ARE HEALED." THAT'S WHY WE ARE TO CALL ON JESUS FOR ANY TYPE OF HEALING, WE NEED IN OUR LIFE WHETHER PHYSICAL, MENTAL, FINANCIALLY, SPIRITUALLY, AND EMOTIONAL. THIS IS A TRUE TESTIMONY I WAS UP EARLY ONE MORNING WITH MENSTRUAL PAIN AND, I DID NOT PRAY AT FIRST. HOWEVER, I WENT BACK TO SLEEP AND WAS AWAKEN SUDDENLY BY THE HOLY GHOST, AND THE PAIN WAS WORST. THEN I REALLY STARTED TO CRY FOR HELP FROM THE LORD NOT JUST FOR MYSELF, BUT ALSO FOR OTHERS WHO MIGHT BE GOING THROUGH THE SAME PAIN I WAS GOING THROUGH. THEN THE LORD LED ME TO PRAY FOR ALL SORTS OF PAIN FOR OTHERS. FINALLY, I ASKED THE LORD TO SING FOR ME AND HE BLESSES ME WITH THIS SONG. OH BOY DID I ENJOY SINGING IT AND I GOT MY HEALING.

"I AM IN LOVE WITH JESUS"

I AM IN LOVE WITH JESUS.
HE STOLE MY HEART
ONE SWEET SEPTEMBER DAY.
WHEN I GAVE MY HEART TO HIM,
IN WATER BAPTISM.
THEN NOT LONG AFTER,
ON A EASTER SUNDAY,
JESUS TOUCH ME AND MADE ME WHOLE.
AND JESUS,
SHOWED ME THE LIGHT, SO BRIGHT.
I WAS KNOCKED OF MY FEET,
BY THE POWER OF THE HOLY GHOST.
THEN LATER THAT EVENING,
JESUS TOLD ME ABOUT LOST SOULS.
THAT NEEDED TO BE SAVED.
AND I ANSWERED THE CALL,
THAT'S WHY I AM SINGING THIS SONG,
ABOUT JESUS LOVE FOR ME.
I AM IN LOVE WITH JESUS,
THAT'S WHY I AM IN LOVE WITH JESUS.

I AM IN LOVE WITH JESUS.
HE STOLE MY HEART.
JESUS STOLE MY HEART.
THAT IS WHY I AM IN LOVE WITH JESUS.

33

34

INSPIRED BY GOD'S LOVE, ABUNDANT GRACE FOR ME TO REACH LOST
SOUL FOR HIS KINGDOM. THANK YOU, MY BELOVED FATHER.

"I AM PHOTOGENIC"

2/21/08
3:00 A.M.

I AM PHOTOGENIC,
I DON'T NEED ANY MAKE-UP.
JESUS
GAVE ME BEAUTY FOR ASHES
WHEN HE MARRY ME.
I AM BEAUTIFUL FROM THE INSIDE OUT.
I AM PHOTOGENIC
I AM BEAUTIFIED BY GOD'S SALVATION.
I AM POTOGENIC,
BECAUSE I AM THE MEEK.
I AM PHOTOGENIC.
I AM PHOTOGENIC.
I AM PHOTOGENIC
I AM PHOTOGENIC I DON'T NEED ANY MAKE-UP.
JESUS GAVE ME BEAUTY FOR ASHES.
WHEN HE MARRY ME.
I AM PHOTOGENIC.
I AM PHOTOGENIC.
I AMPHOTOGENIC.

INSPIRED ON 2/21/08, AT 7:30 AM, IN THE SHOWER WHILE I WAS TALKING TO JESUS ABOUT ME GETTING MARRIED ONE DAY IF IT'S HIS WILL, AND BEING THE ONLY BRIDE PROBABLY EVER NOT TO WEAR MAKE-UP ON HER WEDDING DAY! BECAUSE ALL BRIDES I KNOW WEAR MAKEUP ON THE DAY OF THEIR WEDDING, WHETHER THEY ARE SAVED OR NOT. THEN THE LORD SPIN ME AROUND 7 TIMES IN THE TUB AND R EMINE ME THAT I AM BEAUTIFUL AND PHOTOGENIC WITHOUT ANY MAKEUP.

OCEAN CITY NEW JERSEY

Song

<u>God said PRAY</u>

If my people, which are called by my name,
shall humble themselves,
and pray and seek my face,
and turn from their wicked ways:
then will I hear from heaven
and will forgive their sins,
and will heal their land
humble themselves
humble themselves
humble themselves
pray, pray, pray
pray, pray, pray

heal their land
heal their land
heal their land

"BY FAITH"

2/22/08
8:16 A.M.

BY FAITH I AM LIVING.
BY FAITH I AM MOVING.
BY FAITH I AM COOKING.
BY FAITH I AM UNPACKING
NOT KNOWING IF I AM ABLE TO PAY MY MORTGAGE.
LORD, BY FAITH I AM LOVING.
BY FAITH I AM FORGIVING.
BY FAITH I PRAY FOR THE LORD JESUS TO PAY MY MORTGAGE.
BY FAITH, BY FAITH, BY FAITH.
I AM LIVING.
BECAUSE JESUS SAID IN "PSALM 21 THAT HE NEITHER SLEEP NOR
SLUMBER".
BY FAITH, BY FAITH, BY FAITH,
I AM LIVING.
MY HELP COMETH FROM THE LORD WHICH MADE THE HEAVEN AND EARTH.
BY FAITH, BY FAITH, BY FAITH,
I AM DRIVING.
BECAUSE THE LORD TOLD ME THAT HE WILL PRESERVE MY GOING OUT AND
MY COMING IN
FROM THIS TIME FORTH,
AND EVEN FOREVER MORE.

THIS SONG WAS INSPIRED BY GOD ON 8/1/03 IN MOBILE, ALABAMA. AFTER

MOVING THERE AND NOT HAVING A JOB. I HAD TO DEPEND ON GOD TOTALLY

FOR EVERYTHING. EACH TIME I MOVE AND HAD TO RELY ON GOD TO UNPACK MY BELONGINGS, PAY

CAR INSURANCE, SHELTER, FEED ME, WAKE ME UP, AND PROTECT ME. YES, I

HAD TO SLEEP IN MY CAR FOR MORE THAN ONCE DURING MY RELOCATION, BUT

GOD KEPT ME. GOD KEEP THE LANDLORD OFF MY BACK. I HAD TO FAST

WHEN THE RENT WAS DUE AND I HAD NO MONEY. I HAD TO

PRAY TO RELIEVE THE LIFE PRESSURE OF ME.

Thank you, LORD.

"LOOK UP TO JESUS"

DON'T LOOK TO THE LEFT,

NOR TO THE RIGHT.

LOOK UP, LOOK UP, TO JESUS

HE IS THE ONE, WHO WILL STAND BY YOU, AND DELIVER YOU.

LOOK UP, LOOK UP LOOK, LOOK UP TO JESUS.

IN TIMES OF TROUBLE CALL ON JESUS, HE WILL HEAR AND ANSWER YOUR PRAYER.

LOOK UP, LOOK UP, LOOK UP TO JESUS.

DON'T LOOK TO THE LEFT, NOR TO THE RIGHT,

LOOK UP, LOOK UP, LOOK UP TO JESUS!

NO ONE ELSE CAN HELP YOU WHEN TROUBLE (TEMPTATION) IS AT YOUR DOOR.

I WILL LIFT MINE EYES ONTO THE HILLS FROM WHENCE COMETH MY HELP. MY HELP
COMES FROM THE LORD WHICH CREATED THE HEAVEN AND THE EARTH.

THE LADY WITH THE ISSUE OF BLOOD

HE (JESUS) WAS TOUCHED BY HER INFIRMITIES.
WHEN SHE REACH OUT, HER HAND AND TOUCHED THE HEM OF HIS
OUTER GARMENT
SHE HAD BEEN SICK FOR 13, LONG, LONG, YEARS.

AND NO PHYSICIANS COULD SOLVE HER PROBLEM.
YET, JESUS, PRESENCE HEAL HER.
BECAUSE HE WAS TOUCHED BY HER INFIRMITIES.
WHEN SHE REACHED OUT HER HAND.
AND TOUCHED THE HEM OF HIS OUTER GARMENT.
HE (JESUS) WAS TOUCHED BY HER INFIRMITIES.
HE (JESUS) WAS TOUCHED BY HER INFIRMITIES.
HAL-LE-LU-JAH HAL-LE-LU-JAH HAL-LE-LU-JAH!
GLORY! HAL-LE-LU-JAH-GLORY-HAL-LA-LU-JAH!
GLORY! HAL-LE-LU-JAH-GLORY-HAL-LA-LU-JAH!
A MEGA-HIT SONG THIS SHALL BE.
THIS SONG WAS INSPIRED ON 12/29/07
WHILE READING THE BIBLE AT MARGARET'S HOUSE ABOUT JESUS HEALING
MINISTRY AND HOW HE HEALED THE WOMAN WITH THE ISSUE OF BLOOD.
THE COMPASSION JESUS HAD FOR HER WHEN HE REALIZED VIRTUE HAD
GONE OUT OF HIM.

St. Matthew 9:20-22. SAYS, BUT JESUS TURNED HIM ABOUT AND WHEN HE
SAW HER, HE SAID DAUGHTER, BE OF GOOD COMFORT, THY FAITH HATH MADE
THEE WHOLE. AND THE WOMAN WAS MADE WHOLE FROM THAT HOUR.

"SING A NEW SONG ONTO THE LORD"

THE LORD, HE IS MAJESTY AND POWER.

THE LORD GIVES STRENGTH, AND BEAUTY IN HIS CONGREGATION.

OH, CLAP YOUR HAND AND SING ON TO THE LORD A NEW SONG.

THE LORD GIVES STRENGTH, AND BEAUTY IN HIS CONGREGATION.

THE LORD IS MAJESTY AND POWER.

HO, SING ONTO THE LORD HE IS MAJESTY.

THE LORD IS POWER

THE LORD IS POWER.

THE LORD OF HOST IS POWER.

THE LORD OF HOST IS MAJESTY.

THE LORD OF HOST IS MAJESTY.

45

INSPIRED 1/9/07

AFTER A HARD DAY ON THE JOB THE DEVIL JUMPS INTO ELLEN, MY CO-WORKER

WHO SAID I SHOULD NOT BE READING THE BIBLE EVERY DAY ON THE JOB. LATER SHE

SAID SHE WAS GOING TO WRITE ME UP. BUT WHAT SHE DID NOT KNOW WAS
THE BATTLE WAS NOT MINE BUT IT BELONGS TO THE LORD. AFTER I

FINISH READING THE BIBLE AND THE GUIDEPOST TO THE RESIDENTS.

I TOLD HER TO COME AND DO ACTIVITIES SINCE

SHE WAS COMPLAINING, I GOT UP AND SAID THE CHAIR IS YOURS,

THEN SHE SAID I AM GOING TO WRITE YOU UP AGAIN.

I SAID IN MUCH CONFIDENCE IN GOD AND MYSELF

YOU WILL NOT WRITE ME UP.

THE DEVIL IS A LIAR.

I WENT TO CONFRONT HER WITH THE WORD OF GOD IN MY HEART WHEN I SAW

HER IN THE OFFICE COMPLAINING TO ONE OF THE STAFF MEMBERS ABOUT

ME, WHO WAS TELLING HER TO CALM DOWN.

THANK GOD FOR THE VICTORY I WAS

ALSO FASTING. LATER A CO-WORKER SAID TO ME, WHO WAS PRESENT

AT THE TIME OF THE INCIDENT, MARIE IF GOD WANTS YOU TO READ THE

BIBLE HE WILL LET YOU DO IT, THEY COMPLAIN ABOUT YOU BEFORE

AND SEE YOU ARE STILL DOING IT. THANK GOD FOR MY CO-

WORKER'S ENCOURAGEMENT.

"LET THE WEAK SAY I AM STRONG"

LET THE WEAK SAY

I AM STRONG, I AM STRONG.

WHOM GOD HAS DELIVERED,

BECAUSE THE LORD SAID,

HE SATISFIED

THE MEEK WITH SALVATION.

LET THE WEAK SAY I AM STRONG

BECAUSE HE DESIRES US TO OVERCOME.

GOD SHALL STRENGTHEN YOUR FEEBLE MIND WITH HIS LOVE.

LET THE WEAK SAY, I AM STRONG WHOM GOD HAS DELIVERED.

LET THE WEAK SAY I AM STRONG WHOM HE HAD DELIVERED.

3/22/08
11:00 P.M.

"sacrifice"

WHERE WOULD I BE,
IF JESUS HAD NOT BEEN THE ULTIMATE SACRIFICE FOR ME?
LOST AT SEA,
LOST AT SEA,
THANK YOU, LORD.
THANK YOU, LORD, FOR SACRIFICING YOUR LIFE FOR ME.
THANK YOU FOR DYING ON THE CROSS JUST FOR ME.
WHERE WOULD I BE?
IF JESUS HAD NOT BEEN THE FINAL AND ULTIMATE SACRIFICE FOR ME?
LOST AT SEA.
THANK YOU, LORD.
GOD FOR SACRIFICING YOU SON JESUS JUST FOR ME.

11/21, 2008
8:00 A.M.

Sounds

Bow wow, bow wow, the dog can bark.
Ha ha moo moo the cow can moo.
Meow meow meow the cat can say
Neigh neighs neigh the horse neigh.
Isn't it wonderful how God created the animals to play?
Without our creator what would we do?
Bow wow, bow wow, the dog can bark.
Ha ha ha the cow can moo.
Meow meow meow the cat can say.
Neigh neigh neigh the horse neigh.
So, sing and play has the animal do
Bow wow, bow wow, bow wow, the dog can bark.
Ha ha moo moo the cow can moo.
Meow meow meow the cat can say.
Neigh neigh neigh the horse neigh.

God Said the Best Is Yet To Come

8/15/15
2:30 P.M.

Success is all over my life.

Favor is all over my life.

Favor is all over your life.

Yes, God's good hand of favor is all over my life.

That's why God said the best is yet to come.

If I think I have lived for Christ, well the best is yet to come.

Let me tell you, the best is yet to come because favor is all over my life.

This song was inspired in the upper room conference at Bishop Faulkner church, I had just published my first book and was going through some heavy opposition as well as sickness. When God sends His words of encouragement and deliverance to heal me.

God Said "It Is Working Out For My Good"

4/1/2021
10:00 A.M.

My healing is here today and forever.

It is here, God said all my challenges, hindrances, and obstacles,
I have been through healing is here for me.

He has worked it out for my good.

It Is Working Out for My Good.

It Is Working Out for My Good.

It Is Working Out for My Good.

After all I have been through.

It Is Working Out for My Good.

It Is Working Out for My Good.

It Is Working Out for My Good.

After All I Have Been Through

2020
6:15 P.M.

After all I have been through, I did not LOSE MY MIND or be backslidden.

A MIRACLE is coming God said, tomorrow at this time in my life.

A BREAKTHROUGH is coming, no longer will I be oppressed, heartbroken, or despaired.

SUCCESS is all over me God said.

SUCCESS is all over me God said.

And EVERYONE that's CONNECTED to me will be delivered.

LORD, I BELIEVE!

The Needs Of Others

What a delight to help those in need.

It brings such joy and releases to give to those in need.

I feel it to the core of my being.

Fulfilling the need of others, bless my soul when they are satisfied.

I cannot help but give to God's children.

When Jesus was on earth, He took pleasure in helping others.

By healing, feeding, ministering, and raising their dead.

Jesus never fails to go to someone's rescue when they were sick.

His life was such an example to others.

What about yours?

Have you walked in Jesus's footsteps?

If not, why not?

That is why Jesus send us the HOLY GHOST.

WHAT IS YOUR EXCUSE FOR NOT ASSISTING OTHERS!

Delight Your Self In Helping Others

Have you ever considered what it would be like to ASSIST those in your community?

What a delight to HELP those in need.

It brings SUCH JOY and releases to give to those in need.

FULFILLING the need of others bless my soul when they are SATISFIED.

I cannot help but GIVE to God's wonderful people when there is a cry for HELP.

The Faces Of The Needy

4/5/08
7:00 P.M.

They are of all colors, races, and creeds,

Their languages spoken are many.

At times it's difficult to tell what one is saying.

But with a little patience the accent it understood.

They made up a special part of the public's population.

Although they are partly ignored and forgotten about by society.

8/9/08
11:45 P.M.

The Needy In My Community

I wish I could do more for the needy in my community.

I believe it's everyone's moral responsibility to help his or her fellow man in need.

One never knows what may befall them in life!

Life is a struggle and has its difficulties, anyone can become homeless at any moment.

I often think It could have been me when I go to feed the needy.

It's only GOD'S GRACE AND MERCIES that kept me of the streets of America.

Although the Lord has blessed me to achieve a two-college degree, I was
unable to find work while in school and after I graduated.

It was the skills I had prior to and after college that helped me to attain a low-income job.

Jobs, of course, that I was not so delighted to go to at times.

What do I do? when there is a cry for HELP?

I must have compassion and do whatever it takes to ease the hunger of my fellow men.

"That's What Linda Did" LOVE!

11/27/15
4:00 P.M.

Love is not something one expresses after someone they love is dead.

But instead, it is a sincere declaration (expression) to express while one is alive.

That's what Linda did. "LOVE"

The dead cannot hear what one has to say once they are dead,

So, don't make the mistake of waiting till it's too late.

Give love while you can.

That's what Linda did. "LOVE"

Express oneself while one has the time, and opportunity to put in one's time.

That's what Linda did. "LOVE"

Then one's heart won't hurt so bad when one hears their loved one is dead.

Who is to say one will even be allowed to speak at one's homegoing service, only time can tell.

So, take my simple advice and don't wait until it's too late,

Be good to yourself and express ourself before it's too late.

That's what Linda did. "LOVE"

Live and love before it's too late.

That's what Linda did. "LOVE"

That is what God requires of us to do.

That's what Linda did! "LOVE"

Love your neighbor as you love yourself.

That's what Linda did! "LOVE"

Linda, Miss Lin, Granma, Mom has she was affectionately known has,

Always express her love and gratitude to everyone she meets.

She loves without reservation.

So, do has Linda did before it's too late.

Just love.

Just love! It cost you nothing while you have the time.

Love

Love love.

That's what Linda did. "LOVE"

A Gentle Lamb

1/29/2018
2:00 P.M.

A gentle lamb has gone home.

A gentle lamb no more roam.

A gentle lamb no longer speaks.

A gentle lamb no more sing.

A gentle lamb has gone home to be with the Lord.

A gentle lamb who once walked the face of the earth.

A gentle lamb who once bless every heart she meets

A gentle lamb has gone home.

A gentle lamb no more to roam.

A gentle lamb has gone home to be with the Lord.

That's What Linda Did!" LOVE" and A Gentle Lamb are dedicated to my Aunt Linda McBean a true woman of God. One who taught me how to pray has a child. She also taught me how to love and forgive. Linda even taught me the ways of God through her lifestyle. She was a perfect example of Christ's love, from my childhood she has exemplified these characteristic traits until death. I thank God for my Angel Linda McBean, who has left the earth to be with her eternal love and King Jesus Christ forever.

You will always be missed Aunty Linda

THE BLESS FAMILY

Margaret Gordon

4/28/21
4:28 P.M.

Oh, Margret is so sweet.

Oh, how she prays.

Oh, how she loves to intercede.

Oh, how she loves the Lord.

Oh, how she loves to encourage everyone she meets.

Oh, how she loves to be a witness for Jesus.

Oh, Margret is so sweet.

Oh, Margret is so sweet.

Oh, Margret is so sweet.

Margret is the apple of Jesus's eye.

Oh yes, she is the apple of Jesus's eye.

God Is Good To Me

Song

1/ 19 /2019
6:00 A.M.

God is good to me.

God is good to me.

God is good,

God is good,

God is good to me.

God is good to me.

God is good God is good.

God is good to me.

God is good to Chloe.

God is good to Caira

God is good to Esther.

God is good to Coretta.

God is good god is good.

God is good to my whole family.

God said, "He is GOOD to me.

God said, "He is GOOD to my whole family.

God said, "He IS SO GOOD TO ME.

AMEN, AMEN.

68

God says, "I am a Brilliant Baby."

7/ 1/ 2019
8: 00 A.M.

I am a brilliant baby.
I Am A Brilliant Girl.
Jesus brought me into this world for a purpose.
My name is Caria, Caria- Badira
Oh, can't you see take a look at me?
I am a brilliant baby.
I am a brilliant girl.
Jesus brought me into this world for a purpose.
I am a brilliant girl.
I am a brilliant baby.
I am a brilliant girl
I got a leader in me.
Oh, can't you see?
I got a preacher in me
Oh, can't you see?
I got a doctor in me
Oh, can't you see?
I am a BRILLIANT baby
I am a BRILLIANT girl.
I got JESUS IN ME.
I am a brilliant baby.
I am a brilliant girl.

Who Loves Caira!

8/ 8/2020
1:00 P.M.

Who loves Caira?

Who loves Caira?

Mommy loves Caira.

Chloe loves Caira.

Esther loves Caira.

Caria, Caria, Caira

Who loves Caira?

Grandma loves Caria.

Grandpa loves Caira.

Chloe loves Caira.

Caria, Caria, Caira.

Caria, Caria, Caira.

Jesus loves Caira.

Caria, Caria, Caira.

74

Coming Out of The Darkness

4/16/21
10:00 A.M.

Coming out of the darkness

Coming out of the dust

Coming out of the dawn

Coming out of COVID-VIRUS

Coming out of life's much

Coming out of the dust.

Coming out with much

Coming out with JESUS

JESUS is the light.

Coming out of the darkness

Coming out of the dust

Coming out of the dawn

Coming out of COVID-19

Coming out with King Jesus

Coming out with Jesus He is the LIGHT.

COMING OUT WITH JESUS, HE IS THE KING OF KINGS

COMING OUT WITH JESUS HE IS THE LORD OF LORDS

Jesus.

I AM HONORED TO BE YOUR FATHER

11/27/15
4:45 P.M.

Have the Lord ever told you, He is honored to be your Father?

As He ever told you, He appreciated you?

Or trust you?

Well,

it is an honor for me (Esther) to be a child of God.

God has spoken these words to my heart and they brought tears, joy, laughter,
dancing, worshipping, and applause to His thrown, from my heart.

I am grateful He could choose such a one as I.

How honored I was to hear these words, who me! God, the eternal deity, was He really speaking to me?

Me, I am so REJECTED, DESPITE, and LAUGH AT, MOCKED, and CRITICIZE. Just for WORSHIPING GOD!

Me, who! no one recognized or seem to care about.

Or for that matter esteem me.

Me, who has nothing?

Me, so frail and left to die.

Me, who! is so looked down on?

It is I, that He is speaking to?

God Honors me?

Me!

God honors me.

No, No, No, it cannot be me.

Did, I hear you clearly Lord? Is it really You?

Speak Lord thy servant heareth.

Is this Samuel's God's speaking?

Is it Moses God's speaking?

Is It brother Paul's God speaking?

Believe, and He shall speak, He loves His children so much,
and wants us to know how He feels about us.

I Feel Like An Animal Left To Die.

2/6/16
3:30 P.M.

My afflictions left me feeling lost without hope

I feel like an animal left to die.

Left out in the cold to die without love

I feel like an animal left to die.

Too much heartache and pain.

I can't even see out of my spiritual eye.

I feel like an animal left to die.

Why does it pain me so?

I feel like an animal left to die.

Hay Lord, you promise me peace.

Yet, I feel like an animal in a storm without any help.

I feel like an animal left to die.

Pain in my soul, no one to turn to

I feel like an animal left to die.

I Do Not Fear Death

2/6/16
1:00 P.M.

Death is obvious.

Death stares you in the face every day.

I do not fear death.

Death is inevitable.

Death is sure.

Yet I do not fear death

God says in His word it's appointed to man once to die and after the judgment.

So why should I fear death?

Death is only the beginning of eternal life with God.

So why not welcome your old friend's death it is a promise like everything else from the Lord

So why, why should I fear death?

I do not fear death.

Steady As A Rock

2/6/16

7:00 P.M.

I am steady as my rock.

My rock is Jesus.

My rock dwells in me.

I am steady as a rock.

He flows in me rivers of living water.

He speaks mystery to my ears.

My rock is Jesus.

The rock is steady.

I am steady as my rock.

Rocky steady I am as Jesus.

My rock is Jesus.

I May Not Be A Racehorse

2/6/16

8:30 P.M.

The race is neither for the swift nor the battle for the
strong, but for those that endure to the end.
I may not be a racehorse.
But I must continue with the Christian journey I started with Christ.
I may not be a racehorse.
It may be I must crawl at times to do God's will.
But so be it.
I have come to the conclusion, that I am not a racehorse.
And God does not require me to be one.
Just endure!
Just endure!
Just endure!
Jesus says just endure.
That's how I am going to be saved.

POEM

<u>My Huma! my Huma!</u>

<u>4:40 P.M.</u>

My Huma took such good care of me when I was a child.

She bath, teach and feed me.

Huma was so, patient with me.

She sat me down by her side on a wooden bench while she beats coffee to sell on the streets.

My Huma! My Huma!

Who keeps a close watch on me, just so no one would harm me.

God was her strength and guide.

And protection, she loves to listen to her older granddaughter read the Holy Bible to her.

My Huma loves God, she worships Him in the open field.

My Huma! My Huma!

So old and bent.

Was given the responsibility to take her off me,

When she should be spending her later years in a rocking chair.

My Huma! My Huma!

So faithfully wait.

Waiting for her Lord and Savior Jesus to call her home.

JUSTICE

2/2/15

12:00 P.M.

Justice demands that I serve you.

Justice demands that I serve you.

Oh, justice oh justice.

Oh, where is my life?

Oh, justice give me back my life!

Oh justice, oh justice.

Justice demands that I serve you, Lord.

87

Silent River

4/2/16

11:00 A.M.

The water stood so still.

Yet it seems to be full of life.

It seems to take deep breaths as people do.

How can it be?

Did God create water with life?

Does water really breathe?

Or is it just my imagination running wild?

As I stood by the lakes, oh, the water looks so great and seemed full of life.

Open my eyes Lord

Open and I will come in and sup with them.

Open the doors of my heart Lord.

Open the doors of my heart Lord.

I want you to come in and sup with me.

Open the doors of my heart Lord.

I want you to come in and sup with you.

Lord, I open the doors of my heart to you.

So, you can come in and sup with me.

POEM

1/12/2017

10:00 P.M.

My Huma! my Huma!

She sat me down by her side on a wooden bench while she beats
coffee to sell on the streets and markets so sweet.

My Huma! My Huma!

Who keeps a close watch on me just so no one would harm me

My Huma! My Huma!

So old and bent

Was given the responsibility to take her off me,

When she should be spending her later years in a rocking chair.

My Huma My Huma

So faithfully waits

Waiting` for her Lord and Savior Jesus to call her home.

Oh, give thanks to the Lord above.

Who provides me with someone to love.

My Huma oh I love and miss you so.

There will never be another one like you.

My Huma, my Huma.

Silent River

4/2/16

8:38 P.M.

The water stood so still.

Yet it seems to be full of life.

It seems to take deep breaths as people do.

How can it be?

Did God create water with life?

Does water really breathe?

Or is it just my imagination running wild?

You Can't Be Like Me

1/6/18

11:47 P.M.

You said you want to be like me.

Don't you pray, and asked God to look like me!

Don't you pray, and asked God to worship like me!

Or sing like me!

Or pray like me!

Or dance like me!

Don't you pray and asked God for the gifts, He has given to me!

Don't you!

Don't you dare, because you don't know what it cost for me to get there?

Don't you dare?

Oh Master

1/6/2018

9:56 P.M.

Oh, master, here are the hands You have given to me.

To use this morning,

They have done so many things I can't count them all

Oh, master dear, here is the feet You have given to me, they have danced so many steps.

I can't even rehearse them all.

Oh, master dear.

Oh, master here is the worship you have enveloped in me!

Here master

Here master is the love You have bestowed upon me!

Please take your gift of love back its too much for me to continue with!

Here master,

Here master,

Here are your blessings You have given to me.

Don't Pity Me

1/6/2018
10:08 P.M.

Don't you pity me!
Just wait, and see what God is going to birth out of me!
I don't want your pity.
Don't you pity me.
Just pray
And let the Lord have His way.
Love is helping,
Love is giving,
Love is praying with compassion.
I don't want your pity.
Lord, I don't want any pity from anyone.
Especially from my enemies.
I have not been where you have been.
Don't you tell me those words?
I don't want your pity, please.
Just pray!
Just pray!
Don't pity me even if I am a church mouse,
because I am a child of God.
Don't you, pity me because Jesus don't.
He just loves me.
No matter what my state or condition.
Just pray, Jesus will deliver me.
Just pray!
Don't you pity me!
Don't you pity me?
I have not been where you have been.
All I do is pray.

I Am Not Crazy

You call me crazy?

God will show you crazy!

When you don't understand what He is doing or manifesting in and through my life.

You call me crazy?

Don't you call me crazy! Because it's the God in me you are calling crazy?

Don't you see?

It's God who lives in me?

He is the one who is worshiping through me!

Don't you ever call me crazy!

Don't you know it affects me?

I am a child of God, not because I worship different from you!

Look! Look! closely and you will see?

See, Jesus in me, the one who died for me and you!

Don't you ever call me crazy, don't you know God see, and hear you?

And He is not, please!

God knows you! Don't you ever call me crazy.

Don't you ever call me crazy.

98

Silent River

4/2/16

1:30 P.M.

The water stood so still.

Yet, it seems to be full of life.

It seems to take deep breaths as people do.

How can it be?

Did God create water with life?

Does water really breathe?

Or is it just my imagination running wild?

As I stood by the lake, oh, the water looks so great, and seems full of life.

Can this really, really be?

Water has life.

Oh Jesus Christ!

You Might As Well Call Me Glory

1/9/2018

5:19 P.M.

You might as well call me Glory because the Glory of God is in me.

I am the glory of God, I am God's Glory.

I was made for the Glory of God.

I am God's dancing Glory.

I am God's smiling Glory.

I am God's laughing Glory.

I am God's shining Glory.

I am God's singing Glory.

I am God's writing Glory.

I am God's speaking Glory.

I am God brake-out Glory.

I am God's breakthrough Glory.

I am God's worshiping Glory.

I was created for the Glory of God.

Oh, what a Glory!

Oh, what a Glory!

Oh, what a Glory!

Are you the Glory of Almighty God?

READER'S NOTE

_____

_____

_____

_____

_____

_____

_____

_____

_____

_____

I am Going Up With Jesus

8/ 6/2017

6:00 P.M.

I am going up with Jesus, praising the Lord.
Singing, shouting, praising the Lord.
I am going up full of the Holy Ghost to be with my Lord.
I am going up to GLORY praise the Lord.
Going up, going up, praise the Lord, singing, and shouting praise the Lord.
I am going to Glory praise the Lord.
I am going to Glory, Glory, Glory praise the Lord.

With My Whole Heart, I Will Serve You Oh Lord

8/18/2016

4:00 P.M.

Hallelujah, hallelujah, hallelujah.
I will praise you; I will praise you; I will praise you.
Oh Jesus!
I will worship you; I will worship you; I will worship you.
Oh Jesus!
I will serve you; I will serve you; I will serve you.
Oh Jesus!
Hallelujah, hallelujah, hallelujah.

Song

I Am An Instrument For Jesus

8/9/2014
7:39 P.M.

I am an instrument.

Design and preserved to show froth the GLOR-Y of God.

God said, "I am an instrument" "made for His Glory."

I am the instrument, God made me to be, to show forth His Glory.

I am an instrument created by God.

To show forth His GLOR-Y!

To show forth His GLOR-Y!

To show forth His GLOR-Y!

To show forth His GLOR-Y!

God says," I am an instrument" an instrument.

An instrument, an instrument created to show forth His GLOR-Y.

To show forth His Glory!

To show forth His Glory!

POEMS

I Open My Heart To The Lord Jesus

5/4/2013
9:00 P.M.

Those who open their heart's Jesus said, I will come in and sup with them.

Open the doors of my heart Lord.

Open the doors of my heart Lord.

I want you to come in and sup with me.

Open the doors of my heart Lord Jesus.

I want you to come in and sup with me.

Lord, I open the doors of my heart to you.

So, you can come in and sup with me.

I open the doors of my heart to You, Lord.

Poem

My Time To Rise

4/30/21
5:14 P.M.

After all the backstabbing

It's my time to rise.

After all the envy

It's my time to rise.

After all the bitterness

It's my time to rise.

After all the greed and hatred

It's my time to rise.

After all the criticism and hypocrisy

It's my time to rise.

God said rise and SHINE and give Him all the GLORY.

IT'S MY TIME TO RISE.

RISE

RISE, RISE, AND SHINE.

Song

THE ANOINTING

5/1/21 5 P.M.
10:00 A.M.

The anointing is falling.

The anointing is falling.

The anointing is falling.

The anointing of God is falling.

The anointing of God is falling.

The anointing is falling.

The anointing is falling.

Because God is on the line.

The anointing of God is falling on me.

It's falling on me, the anointing of God is raining on me.

The anointing is falling.

The anointing is falling.

The anointing of Almighty God is falling on me.

Oh, it's falling.

Oh, it's falling.

It's falling on me.

Song

I Am A Lover of God

5/9/2020
7:00 P.M.

I am a lover of God.

Darkness may rise.

Sickness may call, but I will stand my ground.

I am a lover of God.

I am a child of the King.

Joint heir with Him.

Oh, darkness may come, and sickness may fall.

But I will stand with the King, the King of Kings.

I will testify.

I will testify the truth of God.

I am a lover of God.

The Almighty God the deity God, the one and only God.

Oh, darkness may come, and sickness may fall.

But I am a lover of God, praise God that is who I am.

I am a lover of God.

Oh, can't you see?

There is no one else, out there for me.

I am a lover of God.

I will testify oh comes what may.

I am a lover of God.

I am a child of the King.

I am a lover of God and join heir with him.

I am a lover of God.

I am a lover of God.

Joint heir with Him.

I am a child of the King I will testify.

I am a lover of God.

I am a lover of God.

I am a lover of the King, no matter what come I will dwell with Him.

I am a lover of God.

I am a lover of God.

I am a lover of God.

I am a lover of God.

Though sickness may come I stay with the King.

I am bought with a price, that I can't repay.

I am a lover of the King and join heir with him.

His name is Jesus, His name is Jesus.

His name is Jesus, His name is Jesus.

My KING, I am a lover of God.

I am a lover of God.

I am a lover of God.

Song

<u>Fight For Your Rights</u>

<u>6/5/2017</u>
<u>7:30 P.M.</u>

Fight for your rights.

Speak for your rights. Speak,

speak for your rights and what you have been through.

You have to speak speak for your rights.

If you haven't speak, speak for your rights.

Who would have known what you have been through?

If you haven't fight. Fight for your rights

If you haven't cry, cry, for your rights.

Who would have known what you have been through.

If you haven't speak, speak for your rights.

Who would have known what you have been through?

If you haven't speak, speak for your rights.

Who would have known what you have been through?

If you haven't speak, speak for your rights.

Who would have known what you have been through.

If you haven't cry, cry, for your rights.

Who would have known what you have been through.

If you haven't cry, cry, for your rights.

Who would have known what you have been through.

If you have not speak for yourself, then you would not be alive today.

If you hadn't speak-up, you wouldn't be alive.

If you had not speak-up speak-up for you rights.

Then you would not be alive today.

If you had not fight for your rights.

If you had not fight for your right.

Who would have known what you have been through?

Turn It A Round Lord

<u>**9/3/2019**</u>
<u>**4:00 P.M.**</u>

Turn it around Lord.

Turn it around Lord.

Turn it around.

God has a way of turning it around.

Turning it around, turning it around.

God has a way of turning it around to defy the enemy.

God has a way of turning it around.

Turn it around Lord.

Turn it around Lord.

Turn it around.

God has a way of delivering me by His prophecy.

Oh, God has a way of turning my situation around.

Oh, God has a way of turning it around, delivering me, healing me, sanctifying me,

My God has a way of turning it around.

Just to BLESS ME.

Oh, glory, glory, glory, to God, I praise Him.

Glory, glory, to God, Almighty.

Oh God has a way of turning my situation around.

To deliver me.

Oh, God has a way of turning it around.

Oh, God has a way of turning it around.

Oh God has a way of turning it around to deliver me.

Deliver me Lord.

Deliver me Lord.

Heal me Lord.

Heal me Lord.

Oh God has a way of turning it around.

Turning me around,

Turning me around.

God has a way of turning me around from my enemy.

My God has a way of delivering me.

My God has a way of delivering me.

My God has a way of healing me from myself.

Healing me from people, sickness, and disease.

He is covering me. My God has a way of breaking me out,
breaking me through, and covering me from my enemy.

My God has a way of breaking me out, breaking me
through, and covering me from my enemy.

He is turning it around now.

Turning it around in every situation.

My God has a way of breaking me out of captivity.

Oh God has a way of turning it around, turn it around Lord,

I would like to see you deliver me like Esther in the Bible and the
Jewish people. God, you have a way of bringing me out.

Bringing me out, bringing me out from my enemy.

Turn it around Lord.

Turn it around Lord.

Turn it around Lord.

It Is Well With My Soul

5/1/2021
9:30 A.M.

God said it is well with my soul.

Oh, thank you, Jesus.

There is no other consolation,

revelation, manifestation, or justification,

you can get when God said it is well with my soul.

My soul needs Jesus, oh glory to God.

My heart needs Jesus.

My pancreas needs Jesus.

My heart needs Jesus.

God said it is well with my soul.

What do you do, oh glory to God?

But walk on in faith, oh glory to God.

If God says it is well with your health, oh glory to God Hallelujah.

You take it and give Him a laugh, oh glory to God.

Do you know why I am here?

I am here to make my King Jesus SMILE.

And He is here to make me laugh and worship Him.

God said it is well with my soul.

It is well with my soul because God, Himself has made me whole.

Did you know, oh glory to God that God said it is well with my soul?

Oh, glory to God.

Not man, Not me.

He has made me whole.

Oh, glory to God.

It is well with my soul.

It is well with my soul because God said it is well.

Oh, glory to God hallelujah.

THE BREAKER

5/1/21
9:35 A.M.

Did you know the Breaker is here?

His name is JESUS.

Jesus is here to break every chain.

Every fetter, every barrier.

Did you know the breaker is here?

Jesus is here to remove everything that stops you.

Blocks and hinder you from your destiny.

Did you realize oh glory to God, the breaker stops at your home?

Stop on the job, stops in the street?

And helps everyone he meets.

Did you know the breaker is here?

the breaker is JESUS.

He is here to break down barriers, walls, and fences.

He is here to break down my God's ignorance, hate and malice.

He is here to break down jealousy and pride.

Did you know the breaker is here?

He is here to remove and break down discrimination.

His name is JESUS.

He is a oneness lover, He loves unity, strength, and peace.

Did you know the breaker is here? He abides within you.

Oh, glory to God, hallelujah.

Thank you, Jesus, thank you, Jesus.

Thank you, Jesus, thank you, Jesus.

Thank you, Jesus, thank you, Jesus.

Thank you, Jesus, thank you, Jesus.

Thank you, Jesus, thank you, Jesus.

Hallelujah, hallelujah.

Hallelujah, hallelujah.

The breaker is here.

The breaker is here.

The breaker is here.

Do you have anything to BREAK- DOWN?

Prolific

5/1/2021
9:40 A.M.

God is good to me.

God says prolific to me.

While I was busy working on his work, you see.

Prolific means to be fruitful and productive.

Glory to God, God wants me to be prolific.

In order to be prolific, oh glory to God.

I have to let God produce through me.

God wants me to be fruitful and produce an abundance of literature.

For such a time as this, glory to God.

God is good to me that is what he said.

every morning he wakes me up.

He says he is good to my family.

You see God is good to me.

Not only to me but to my entire family.

Oh, glory to God.

Can God be good to you?

Just you wait and spend a little time with Him.

and you will see.

He is so good to me oh glory to God.

Prolific, you must see, oh glory to God.

Bursting out of me, God says He so good to me.

Oh, glory to God just you wait and see.

God says I am prolific hallelujah just you wait and see.

God has nothing but blessings in store for me hallelujah.

God has nothing but happiness, joy, and peace.

hallelujah is in store for me.

Prolific bursting with laughter, bursting with hugs, and kisses.

To my heavenly Father.

Prolific in these days of COVID-19 virus.

I will be prolific oh glory to God,

just to bless God and His people.

prolific, God said be fruitful and multiply my child,

Bless those you see bless those you do not see.

Oh, glory to God prolific you will be.

<u>LIVE</u>

<u>**5/1/21**</u>
<u>**3:45 P.M.**</u>

Thank you, Jesus, what does it mean to truly live?

Live in this life, oh my goodness, especially with COVID-VIRUS

all around you and the smell of death. Oh, glory to God.

People are on ventilators.

People my goodness with mask.

People do not know how long their lives will last!

What does it mean to live?

Everyday I wake up the Lord is telling me to live.

But dear Lord teach me do teach me how I live. Glory to God.

Hallelujah, when so many lives are lost.

Teach me, Lord, teach me to live.

If You Had Create Me To Be A Tree

5/1/21
9:40 A.M.

At least if you created me to be a tree

I would not feel pain in me.

At least if you create me to be a tree, they would chop me down and build a house.

At least if you created me to be a tree.

I would be standing firm as a pillar in a house.

But I would not be feeling rejected or pain or abused.

At least if you created me to be a tree.

I would not be sick and wouldn't know when my loved ones have died.

At least God if you create me to be a tree.

My leaves could blow, blow, and blow.

At least if you created me to be a tree.

I wouldn't be goodness alone.

I wouldn't know what it's like to be lonely.

Sad or cry or not even die oh glory to God.

At least if you created me to be a tree.

Oh Lord, not even a bee could sting me.

At least if you created me to be a tree.

They may dig me out from my root to build a house.

By building a house I would be helping someone.

At least if you created me to be a tree.

I would be free, free, free.

Free has a bird.

At least if you created me to be a tree.

I could oh my goodness be shelter or a house to live in.

I wouldn't have to work.

I wouldn't need a doctor.

And I wouldn't have to drive a car.

I wouldn't oh glory to God have to talk to anyone.

Glory to God hallelujah.

I would already have my own house and my own
companions would be around me in the forest.

At least if you created me to be a tree.

Oh, glory to God I could be the best I could ever be just for you, love Esther.

Song

It Is Enough

It is enough that Jesus cares about me.

When I don't have a friend to lean on

or call.

God says it is enough that Jesus cares

When all around me is devastation.

God says it is enough that Jesus cares.

When hardship and hypocrites turn their backs on me.

God said it is enough that Jesus cares.

So, why not look to him in times of despair?

because it is enough that Jesus cares.

I am Holy

6/3/2021
7:10 P.M.

I am holy just as Jesus is Holy.

My HEART is holy.

My LIVER is holy.

My EARS are holy.

My kidneys is holy.

My lungs are holy.

My lungs are holy.

My MIND Is holy.

My, SOUL is holy.

My SPIRIT is holy.

I am holy, holy holy.

Jesus say be he, HOLY for I am holy.

I am holy, my LEGS are holy.

My CONVERSATIONS are holy.

My LIPS are holy.

Rosey

5/2//21

9:00 P.M.

Hi Rosey, you, beautiful, beautiful, beautiful tree.

You are looking at me.

As beautiful has can be.

Rosey, Rosey, I can't believe you are my tree.

In the winter you were so naked without a leaf or bud. But look at you now Rosey you are beautiful. Spreading, and blooming.

Rosey, Rosey, Rosey you are looking at me.

Rosey, Rosey, Rosey, I can see the process you have gone through in the winter has paid off in the SPRING.

ROSEY, ROSEY, I AM GOING TO BE JUST LIKE YOU flourishing in everything, GLORY TO GOD.

Rosey, Rosey, I am going to be GLORY TO GOD flourishing, and everything I put my hands to, my voice to, my thoughts OH GLORY TO GOD, will prosper.

ROSEY, ROSEY LOOKING AT ME.

I THANK GOD FOR MY BEAUTIFUL TREE.

OH, GLORY TO GOD!

You keep me Rosey in the summer.

In the winter.

In the spring.

In the fall you have been with me.

God has given you to me as my company.

Rosey, Rosey, Rosey, you, beautiful tree.

I love you.

God bless you.

I Love You

5/5/21
9:35 10:45 A.M.

I love you, I love you, I love you I do.

I love you, I love you, I love you I do.

I love you, I love you, I love you I do.

I love you, I love you, I love you I do.

Who will go, who will go, who will go.

I love you, I love you, I love you I do.

I love you, I love you, I love you I do.

I love you, I love you, I love you I do.

I love you, I love you, I love you I do.

Who will go, who will go, who will go.

I love you, I love you, I love you I do.

I love you, I love you, I love you I do.

I love you, I love you, I love you I do.

I love you, I love you, I love you I do.

HE LIVES CHRIST JESUS LIVES IN ME!

All poems are inspired and motivated by the power of the Holy Ghost. It gives me great pleasure to share my poetry, songs, and gifts with a wonderful audience of all nations in this 21st century. My desire is that by reading these poems one's spirit would be uplifted. In essence, one would also captivate the beauty of their God-given gifts, and abilities. Thus, bringing forth many fruits in their due season.

Printed in the United States
by Baker & Taylor Publisher Services